Buddhism and the West :
The Integration of Buddhism into Western Society

For thirty-five years Sangharakshita has been playing an important part in the spread of Buddhism throughout the modern world. He is head of the Western Buddhist Order (Trailokya Bauddha Mahasangha), and is actively engaged in what is now an international Buddhist movement with centres in thirteen countries worldwide. When not visiting centres he is based at a community in Norfolk. His writings are available in eleven languages.

Also by Sangharakshita:
A Survey of Buddhism
Flame in Darkness
The Enchanted Heart
The Three Jewels
Crossing the Stream
The Essence of Zen
The Path of the Inner Life
The Thousand-Petalled Lotus
Human Enlightenment
The Religion of Art
The Ten Pillars of Buddhism
The Eternal Legacy
Travel Letters
Alternative Traditions
Conquering New Worlds
Ambedkar and Buddhism
The History of My Going for Refuge
The Taste of Freedom
New Currents in Western Buddhism
A Guide to the Buddhist Path
Learning to Walk
Vision and Transformation
The Buddha's Victory
Facing Mount Kanchenjunga
The FWBO and 'Protestant Buddhism'

The Meaning of Orthodoxy in Buddhism
Mind—Reactive and Creative
Aspects of Buddhist Morality
Buddhism and Blasphemy
Buddhism, World Peace, and Nuclear War
The Bodhisattva: Evolution and Self-Transcendence
The Glory of the Literary World
Going For Refuge
The Caves of Bhaja
My Relation to the Order
Hercules and the Birds and Other Poems

Sangharakshita

Buddhism and the West :
The Integration of Buddhism into Western Society

WINDHORSE PUBLICATIONS

Published by Windhorse Publications
136 Renfield Street
Glasgow G2 3AU

© Sangharakshita 1992
Cover design Dhammarati

Printed by F. Crowes & Sons Ltd,
Norwich

British Library Cataloguing in Publication Data
A catalogue record for this book is available from the British Library

ISBN 0-904766-55-1

The Integration of Buddhism into Western Society

'THE INTEGRATION OF BUDDHISM into Western Society' is a very big subject.
To begin with, Buddhism is very big subject in itself, and it would
hardly be possible to speak of the integration of Buddhism into Western
society, or into anything else, without first explaining what one
understood by the term Buddhism. Is Buddhism a religion, or a
philosophy, or a system of ethics, or is it something quite different from
any of these? Is it, perhaps, something for which there is no word in our
modern Western languages? Does Buddhism exist independently of the
various Eastern Buddhist cultures in which it is historically embodied, or
is it distinguishable and separable from them? In order to be a Buddhist
does one have to transform oneself into a Tibetan, or a Japanese, or a
Thai, in accordance with the particular sectarian form of Buddhism one
wishes to adopt? Then there is the subject of Western society. That too
is a very big subject. Society is 'a system of human organizations
generating distinctive cultural patterns and institutions and usually
providing protection, security, continuity, and a national identity for its
members.' As such, society has a cultural, an economic, a legal, and a
political dimension, and if one was to speak of the integration of
Buddhism into Western society one would have to deal with its
integration in respect of each of these dimensions. Finally, there is the
subject of integration which, though not as big a subject as either
Buddhism or society, is yet big enough. By the integration of Buddhism
into Western society does one mean its bodily incorporation into that

society, unchanged, and without its bringing about any change in that society, or does one mean its diffusion throughout Western society?

Thus the subject of the integration of Buddhism into Western society is a very big one, but the organizers of this Congress, besides asking me to speak on it, have allotted me some forty-five or fifty minutes in which to do so. Either they underestimated the dimensions of the subject or overestimated my ability to deal with it in the time allotted. It would be pleasant to think that the latter alternative was the case, but if this is so then I am going to have to disappoint our good organizers, and must ask them and you to forgive me. I am quite unable to deal with the subject of 'The Integration of Buddhism into Western Society' systematically in the space of some forty-five or fifty minutes. Therefore I shall deal with it unsystematically, not to say subjectively. I shall deal with it by telling you the story of my own interaction with Western society, after I had spent twenty years in the East, in the hope that this will shed at least some light on the very big subject of 'The Integration of Buddhism into Western Society'.

In left England in 1944, a few days before my nineteenth birthday. By that time I was already a Buddhist, having discovered Buddhism when I was sixteen or seventeen and having at once realized that I was, in fact, a Buddhist and always had been. In 1943, the fourth year of the war, I was conscripted into the army, despite my having spent much of my childhood as an invalid, and the following year I was posted to India, the land of the Buddha. There followed postings to Ceylon (Sri Lanka) and to Singapore. In 1947, the war having ended, I left the army and spent two years in South India as a free-lance wandering ascetic. At the end of that period I received the lower ordination as a Buddhist monk and the following year, 1950, the higher ordination. During the seventeen years from 1947 to 1964 I studied with Indian, Tibetan, and Chinese Buddhist teachers, meditated, and wrote and lectured on the Dharma, all the time remaining in India and leading the simple life of a Buddhist monk and becoming increasingly Indianized.

1964 saw a dramatic change. In that year I returned to England for what was originally intended to be a short visit, and in 1967, having paid a farewell visit to my teachers and disciples in India, I returned to England for good and started a new Buddhist movement, the Friends of the Western Buddhist Order. Thus after twenty years in the East, seventeen of them as a monk, I was interacting with Western society. That society seemed very strange to me, as it in many ways still does. It was strange to me for two reasons. In the first place, not only had I been leading the simple life of a Buddhist monk; I had also been leading that life within the context of a society with a traditional culture, and Western society was far from having a traditional culture. In the second place, during the twenty years that I had been away Western society had changed, at least English society had changed. Wartime austerity had been replaced by postwar prosperity. There were more motor cars on the roads, more telephones, refrigerators, and washing machines in people's homes. There were launderettes and supermarkets—neither of which had I seen before. There was television, with enormous aerials sprouting from the thatched roofs of tiny country cottages. Moreover, manners and morals had changed. People spoke differently, dressed differently, and behaved differently—sometimes in ways that before the war would have would have been considered quite shocking.

This was the society with which I was now interacting. This was the society into which, after my twenty years in the East, I was trying to integrate Buddhism when I started the Friends of the Western Buddhist Order.

The initial point of interaction was meditation. Mind, one could say, started to interact with individual mind. Within weeks of my final return to England I started conducting weekly meditation classes in a tiny basement room in central London, only a few hundred yards from Trafalgar Square. Subsequently I likened this basement room, in which the FWBO began its existence, to the catacombs in which the early Christians took refuge from their persecutors and where they developed their doctrine. In these meditation classes I taught two methods of meditation, the anapana-sati or 'awareness of in-and-out breathing' and metta-bhavana or 'development of loving-kindness' (methods now taught throughout the FWBO), and it was not long before people attending the classes began to experience some of the benefits of these practices. Their minds became calmer and clearer and they felt happier. This was only to be expected. Meditation can be defined, at least provisionally, as the raising of the level of consciousness by working directly on the mind itself, or, alternatively, as the gradual replacement of a succession of unwholesome mental states by a succession of wholesome mental states. Howsoever defined, meditation means change, change for the better, in respect of one's mind, or heart, or consciousness.

Thus the integration of Buddhism into Western society involves, to begin with, raising the level of consciousness of at least some of the people who make up that society. The two methods of meditation I have mentioned are able to raise the level of consciousness only temporarily, but there are other methods, also taught in the FWBO, which are able to raise it permanently, or which are able, alternatively, to replace a succession of unwholesome mental states by a succession of wholesome mental states which, since they are imbued with 'clear vision', will never be replaced by a succession of unwholesome mental states.

When I had been conducting my meditation classes for a few months the FWBO held the first of its retreats. Some fifteen or twenty of us spent a week together in a large house in the countryside, fifty miles from London. We spent part of our time meditating, part of it in devotional practices and discussion. Some people had come because they wanted to deepen their experience of meditation, which with varying degrees of success they were able to do. But this was not all. Without exception, those taking part in the retreat found that simply being away from the city, away from their jobs and families, in the company of other Buddhists, and with nothing to think about except the Dharma, was sufficient to raise their level of consciousness quite dramatically.

Here, then, was another point of interaction. The level of consciousness of the people who make up Western society could be raised not only by meditation, or working directly on the mind itself. It could also be raised by changing the conditions under which they lived. It could be raised by changing the environment. It could be raised, at least to some extent, by changing society. The integration of Buddhism into Western society therefore involves changing Western society. Inasmuch as our level of consciousness is affected by external conditions, it is not enough for us to work directly on the mind itself, through meditation, as though it was possible for us to isolate ourselves from society or to ignore the conditions under which we and others live. We must change Western society, and change it in such a way as to make it easier, or at least less difficult, for us to lead lives dedicated to the Dharma within that society. To the extent that Western society has not been changed by Buddhism, it could be said, to that extent Buddhism has not been integrated into Western society. In order to change Western society it will be necessary for us to create Western Buddhist institutions, Western Buddhist life-styles. I shall have something to say about some of these institutions in a minute.

At the time I was conducting meditation classes and leading retreats, during the first few years of the FWBO's existence, I was delivering public lectures, both under the auspices of the FWBO and at the invitation of universities and other outside bodies. In these lectures I sought to communicate the fundamental ideas or concepts of Buddhism in a way that was both intelligible to a Western audience *and* faithful to the spirit, and even to the letter, of Buddhist tradition. Here was yet another point of interaction with Western society, this time one that was of a more intellectual character. The integration of Buddhism into Western society involves the introduction of Buddhist ideas into Western intellectual discourse. By Buddhist ideas I do not mean the doctrinal refinements of the Abhidharma or the philosophical subtleties of the Madhyamika and Yogachara Schools, though these have begun to attract the attention of professional philosophers and theologians in the West. I am speaking of ideas so fundamental that Buddhists themselves often take them for granted and fail to recognize their full significance. Such, for example, is the idea that religion does not necessarily involve belief in God, the creator and ruler of the universe, and that it is quite possible for one to lead an ethical and spiritual life, and to raise the level of one's consciousness, without invoking the aid of any outside, supernatural power.

If Buddhism is to be integrated into Western society Buddhist ideas of this fundamental kind, which have been known to strike those previously unacquainted with them with the force of a revelation, will have to become familiar to all educated Europeans and Americans. Moreover, we shall have to establish, wherever possible, connections between Buddhist ideas and concepts of Western origin, as I have done in the case of the Buddhist idea of conditionality, mundane and transcendental, and the Western concept of evolution. We shall have to be able to recognize the Buddhistic nature of some of the insights of Western philosophers, poets, novelists, and dramatists. Goethe, for example, has some interesting comments on self-education and self-transformation—a subject of central importance in Buddhism. The bridge between East and West must be built from both sides.

But to return to Western Buddhist institutions, which we are under the necessity of creating if Western society is to be changed and Buddhism integrated into that society. When the FWBO had held a few retreats, some of the people who had taken part in them regularly started to feel that they wanted to prolong the experience, at least to an extent. Even if they were not in a position to move to the countryside, or give up their jobs (though some did give them up), they wanted to live with other Buddhists and have more time for thinking about the Dharma and, of course, more time for practising it. In this way there came into existence what came to be called residential spiritual communities. The members of these communities did not just live under the same roof. They meditated together every morning, ate together, studied the Dharma together, encouraged one another in their Buddhist life, and contributed to the maintenance of the physical basis of the community. That was twenty or more years ago. Now the FWBO has scores of residential spiritual communities, in a number of countries.

These communities are of several different kinds. Some are quite small, consisting of only four or five persons, while others are relatively large, consisting of anything up to thirty persons. Most are situated in the city, though a few, including some of the largest, are to be found in rural areas. Some community members have outside jobs, while others work within the FWBO. The most successful, and perhaps most typical kind of FWBO spiritual community, is the single sex community consisting of either men only or women only. Mixed sex communities, including those containing families, have not worked very well or lasted very long. Some women's communities, however, contain mothers and children, and this arrangement seems to work. Husbands and wives, as well as lovers, sometimes live in separate, single sex communities.

Thus we change Western society, thereby integrating Buddhism into that society, by creating Western Buddhist institutions, in this case the institution of the residential spiritual community, which to some extent replaces the institution of the nuclear family. The residential spiritual community, as I have described it, is not an Eastern Buddhist institution. In most Buddhist countries society is divided into two mutually exclusive groups, the monastic and the lay, the latter being very much the larger of the two. The FWBO is neither a monastic movement nor a lay movement, and its communities are neither monastic nor lay communities, though some members of some communities are celibate. I shall have more to say about this aspect of the integration of Buddhism into Western society towards the end of this talk.

Another Western Buddhist institution is the team-based right livelihood business, in which the point of interaction with Western society is economic. Some of the people who were living together in FWBO residential spiritual communities, but who had outside jobs, started to feel that they wanted to work together. In some cases this was because their present job was not of a very ethical nature, and

Buddhism attaches great importance to what it terms 'right means of livelihood', the fifth step of the Buddha's noble eightfold path. In others, it was because they did not want to spend their working life in the company of people who were hostile or indifferent to Buddhism or whose behaviour they found offensive. Thus there came into existence the first of what came to be called the FWBO's team-based right livelihood businesses. They were 'team-based' because they consisted of a number of Buddhists working together along broadly co-operative lines, and they were 'right livelihood' because they operated in accordance with Buddhist ethical principles. But there was another factor in their genesis. In 1975 the FWBO embarked on the creation of 'Sukhavati' and the London Buddhist Centre, in east London, at present the second largest of its urban centres. Huge sums of money were needed. Instead of appealing for help to wealthy Buddhists in the East, as other groups might have done, the FWBO raised the money itself, partly by setting up team-based right livelihood businesses which donated their profits to the project. Such businesses thus came to do four things. They provided those working in them with material support, they enabled Buddhists to work with one another, they conducted themselves in accordance with Buddhist ethical principles, and they gave financial support to Buddhist activities.

Over the years the FWBO has set up a number of team-based right livelihood businesses, not all of which have survived. Existing economic institutions are immensely powerful, and the integration of Buddhism into the economic life of Western society is therefore a task of enormous difficulty. In the early days of the FWBO I once did a television interview on Buddhism while walking through the streets of the City, the financial centre of London. Pointing to the Bank of England and the Stock Exchange, I remarked, 'This is what we are up against.' Nonetheless, some of our team-based right livelihood businesses have done extremely well. One of them currently 'employs' more than sixty people and has an annual turnover of £2,000,000.

We can now begin to see what the integration of Buddhism into

Western society actually involves. There is what we may term psychological integration, consisting of the raising of the level of consciousness of at least some of the people who make up that society. The level of consciousness is raised by meditation, or working directly on the mind itself, as well as by various indirect methods such as Hatha Yoga and T'ai Chi Chu'an which I have not had time to mention. Since the level of consciousness is affected by the conditions under which we live, we have to change those conditions, change Western society, and in order to change Western society we shall have to create Western Buddhist institutions. We shall have to create, for example, residential spiritual communities, representing the integration of Buddhism into Western society in the narrower sense of the term, and team-based right livelihood businesses, representing the integration of Buddhism into the economic life of Western society. We shall have to integrate Buddhism into Western society intellectually by introducing its fundamental ideas into Western intellectual discourse and making them, in fact, familiar to all educated Europeans and Americans. Unless we do these things, and many other things of the same kind, there can be no question of any integration of Buddhism into Western society and all talk of such integration will be just so much hot air. But though I have spoken of the psychological, the social, the economic, and the intellectual integration of Buddhism, there is one kind of integration of which I have not spoken, even though it is the most important of all, in the sense that all the other kinds of integration of Buddhism into Western society depend upon it and cannot, in fact, exist without it. Before going on to speak of this kind of integration, however, and therewith begin thinking of bringing this talk to an end, I want to say a few words about a broader kind of integration of Buddhism into Western society.

This broader kind of integration is the integration of Buddhism into Western culture, in the sense of its integration into the whole body of the fine arts, music, and literature. At the beginning of this talk I referred to my returning to England for good in 1967 and founding the FWBO. Earlier this year the FWBO celebrated its twenty-fifth anniversary. The celebrations included the performance of 'Carpe Diem', a Buddhist oratorio by a member of the Western Buddhist Order, and a performance of *A Face Revealed*, a play based on the first four chapters of the *White Lotus Sutra*, written by another Order member. While it would be premature to pronounce upon the intrinsic merits of these works, they undoubtedly constitute points of interaction between Buddhism on the one hand and Western music and drama on the other. They represent the integration of Buddhism into Western culture. There are other points of interaction. Over the years, members of the Western Buddhist Order and their friends have produced Buddha-images and Buddha-icons which, while faithful to the spirit of Buddhist tradition, show a sensitivity to Western aesthetic values. A similar integration of Buddhism into Western culture seems to be taking place, perhaps more sporadically, within certain North American Buddhist circles.

But now for the kind of integration on which all the other kinds of integration of Buddhism into Western society depend, and about which I have not yet spoken. This most important integration of all is the integration of the individual, that is, of the individual Buddhist. It is the individual Buddhist who meditates, who goes on retreat, who lives in a spiritual community or works in a team-based right livelihood businesses, and who communicates the fundamental ideas of Buddhism. It is the individual Buddhist who paints pictures, composes music, writes plays and poems, and sculpts Buddha-images. Without the individual Buddhist there can be no integration of Buddhism into Western society. The idea of such a thing would, indeed, be absurd. But what is a Buddhist?

First of all let me say what a Buddhist is not. A Buddhist is not someone who has simply been born into a Buddhist family, though being born into a Buddhist family obviously does not prevent one from being a Buddhist. A Buddhist is not someone who has made an academic study of Buddhism and has an exhaustive factual knowledge of the history, doctrines, and institutions of Buddhism. Such a person is no more a Buddhist than the director of an art gallery is an artist or, perhaps I should say, than the caretaker of an art gallery is an artist. Similarly, a Buddhist is not someone who merely dabbles in Buddhism, who has a smattering of knowledge about it, who airs purely subjective views on the subject, and who mixes Buddhism up with Christianity, or Vedanta, or New Ageism, or what not. What, then, *is* a Buddhist? A Buddhist is someone who goes for Refuge to the Buddha, the Dharma, and the Sangha, and who, as an expression and as a reinforcement of that Going for Refuge, seeks to observe the ethical precepts of Buddhism.

Going for Refuge to the Buddha means accepting the Buddha, and no other, as one's ultimate spiritual guide and exemplar. Going for Refuge to the Dharma means doing one's utmost to understand, practise, and realize the fundamental import of the Buddha's teaching. Going for Refuge to the Sangha means looking for inspiration and guidance to those followers of the Buddha, both past and present, who are spiritually more advanced than oneself. The ethical precepts that one observes as an expression and as a reinforcement of that threefold Going for Refuge are the precept of reverence for life, the precept of generosity, the precept of contentment, and the precepts of truthful, gracious, helpful and harmonious speech, and so on. The word refuge, which is the literal translation of the original Indic term, is liable to be misunderstood. It does *not* have connotations of running away, or of seeking to escape from the harsh realities of life through losing oneself in pseudo-spiritual fantasies. Rather does it represent (i) the whole-hearted recognition of the fact that permanence, identity, unalloyed bliss, and pure beauty are not to be found anywhere in mundane existence, but only in the transcendental Nirvanic realm, and (ii) the whole-hearted resolve to make the great transition from the one to the other.

Such is the Buddhist. Such is the individual without whom there can be no integration of Buddhism into Western society. But the individual, the individual Buddhist, does not go for Refuge to the Buddha, the Dharma, and the Sangha alone or in isolation. He or she goes for

Refuge in the company of other individuals who also go for Refuge. He or she is a member of the Sangha or spiritual community in the wider sense and it is this Sangha, and not so much the individual Buddhist alone or in isolation, that raises the level of consciousness of people living in Western society, changes that society by creating Western Buddhist institutions, introduces the fundamental ideas of Buddhism into Western intellectual discourse, and interacts with Western fine arts, music, and literature. It is this wider spiritual community that effects the psychological, social, economic, and cultural integration of Buddhism into Western society.

This brings me back to the aspect of the integration of Buddhism into Western society to which I referred earlier on, when I spoke of the FWBO as being neither a monastic movement nor a lay movement. It also brings me very nearly to the end of this talk. At the time that I started the FWBO a Buddhist movement had been in existence in Britain for about fifty years. It was a very small movement, and one of the reasons for its smallness was that it was to a great extent controlled by people who, though sympathetic to Buddhism, were not actually Buddhists, and who could not bring to the work of making known the Dharma the energy and conviction of Buddhists. A year after starting the FWBO I therefore founded not another Buddhist society but a spiritual community, a Sangha, an Order. I founded the Western Buddhist Order or WBO, all the members of which are Buddhists, in that they all go for Refuge to the Buddha, the Dharma, and the Sangha, and undertake to observe the ten fundamental precepts of ethical behaviour. It is this Order that directs FWBO activities and institutions in more than a dozen countries, including Germany, and which I believe offers a paradigm for the integration of Buddhism into Western society. Without such an Order, their common membership of which enables individual Buddhists to co-operate on the closest terms, there can be no integration of Buddhism into Western society such as I have described. It is therefore good to know that membership of the European Buddhist Union, which together with the German Buddhist Union has organized this Congress, is open only to *bona fide* Buddhist organizations whose membership is predominantly Buddhist and whose council or board is under the control of professed Buddhists. This is a move in the right direction and one that augurs well for the future of Buddhism in Europe.

But while there can be no integration of Buddhism into Western society without an Order, equally that Order itself must be an integrated Order in the sense of being without serious internal divisions, that is, divisions between Buddhists of different kinds. It must be a unified Order. The Western Buddhist Order is a unified Order in three important respects. Firstly, it is an Order of Buddhists, that is, of individuals who go for Refuge to the Buddha, the Dharma, and the Sangha, and who undertake to observe the ten ethical precepts. It is neither a monastic Order nor a lay Order, which is why the FWBO is neither a monastic movement nor a lay movement. In the WBO and FWBO commitment, in the sense of Going for Refuge, is primary, and life-style, in the sense of living more as a monk or nun or more as a layman or laywoman, is secondary. This does not mean that life-style is unimportant but only that it is less important than commitment or Going for Refuge, the latter being the central or definitive act of the Buddhist life and as such the fundamental basis of unity and union among Buddhists. Secondly, the Western Buddhist Order is an Order of both men and women, who are admitted on equal terms. Men and women receive the same ordination, engage in the same spiritual practices, and undertake the same organizational responsibilities. Thirdly and lastly, the Western Buddhist Order is not a sectarian Order, in that it does not identify itself with any one form of Buddhism. Instead, it rejoices in the riches of the whole Buddhist tradition and seeks to draw from those riches whatever is of value for its own practice of the Dharma here in the West. Thus the Western Buddhist Order is a unified Order, an integrated Order, and it is because it is an integrated Order that it has been able to make its contribution to the integration of Buddhism into Western society and, indeed, to offer a paradigm for that integration.

As I observed at the beginning of this talk, 'The Integration of Buddhism into Western Society' is a very big subject, and I hope that by telling you the story of my own—and the FWBO's—interaction with Western society I have been able to shed at least some light on it. This Congress is being held in Berlin, and I am addressing you not far from the area which, three years ago, saw the dismantling of a notorious symbol of disunion and disintegration. Happily East and West Berlin, and East and West Germany, are now unified or, as we may say, integrated. We, the Buddhists of Europe and America, are concerned with a different kind of integration—the integration of Buddhism into Western society. Let us therefore do away with our divisions. Let us do away with the divisions between monastic and lay Buddhists, between men and women Buddhists, and between the followers of different sects and schools of Buddhism. Let us have an integrated Buddhism and an integrated Buddhist community. Let us base ourselves firmly and unmistakably upon our common Going for Refuge to the Buddha, the Dharma, and the Sangha.

One last word. I have spoken on the integration of Buddhism into Western society because that is what I was asked to speak on. But as my talk proceeded it will have become obvious to you that what we really have to do is integrate Western society into Buddhism. There is much in Western society that needs changing. Buddhism can help us change it. May this Congress be a step in that direction.

Also from Windhorse Publications

A Guide to the Buddhist Path
Sangharakshita

No matter how enticing the Buddhist path may seem, the modern Westerner will surely hesitate before setting foot upon it. So many schools have evolved over the centuries, so much literature has emerged, and so many people have left their mark on the tradition, that it can be hard even to know what Buddhism actually is. Which teachings really matter? How does one begin to practise Buddhism in a systematic way? This is confusing territory. Without a guide one can easily get dispirited or lost.

In this highly readable anthology a leading Western Buddhist sorts out fact from myth, essence from cultural accident, to reveal the fundamental ideals and teachings of Buddhism. The result is a reliable map of the Buddhist path that anyone can follow. It is just the guide we need.

Sangharakshita is an ideal companion on the path. He is intimately familiar with the various strands of the Buddhist tradition and profoundly experienced in Buddhist practice. As founder of a major Western Buddhist movement he has helped thousands of people to make an effective contact with the richness and beauty of the Buddha's teachings.

256 pages, 246mm x 195mm
ISBN 0 904766 35 7
Paperback £10.95/$21.95

Facing Mount Kanchenjunga
Sangharakshita

In a delightful volume of memoirs, glowing with affection and humour, Sangharakshita shares the incidents, encounters, and insights of his early years in Kalimpong. These include a brush with the Bombay film industry—and several more with the Buddhist 'establishment', a tour with the relics of the Buddha's chief disciples, a meeting with the 'Untouchables'' saviour, Dr B.R. Ambedkar, the discovery of a spiritual kinship with Lama Anagarika Govinda, and much, much more. Behind the events we witness the transformation of a rather eccentric young man—as he must surely have appeared to his fellow expatriates—into a unique and confident individual, completely at home in his adopted world and increasingly effective as an interpreter of Buddhism for a new age.

498 pages, 216mm x 135mm
ISBN 0 904766 52 7
Paperback £11.95/$24.00

The Three Jewels
Sangharakshita

The Three Jewels are living symbols, supreme objects of commitment and devotion in the life of every Buddhist.

The Buddha Jewel: symbol of Enlightenment, particularly as embodied in Siddhartha Gautama, the man who discovered the path to human perfection.

The Dharma Jewel: symbol of the path itself: a host of insights and practical guidelines that help the individual to plot a course towards Enlightenment.

The Sangha Jewel: symbol of the fellowship enjoyed between those whose lives are based on the quest for Enlightenment.

To understand the Three Jewels is to understand the central ideals and principles of Buddhism. To have some insight into them is to touch its very heart.

This book is an authoritative introduction to Buddhist doctrine and philosophy by an outstanding Western Buddhist teacher. Sangharakshita's scholarship makes *The Three Jewels* an essential text for anyone seeking access to the immense riches of a great spiritual tradition.

304 pages, 215mm x 135mm
ISBN 0 904766 49 7
Paperback £8.95/$17.95

For a catalogue of Windhorse books, please write to
Windhorse Publications, 136 Renfield Street, Glasgow G2 3AU, Scotland